I dedicate this book to my Mother

Thank you for always being my biggest supporter
and soucrce of motivation

Preface

Welcome to the ultimate guide on email writing for business!

In today's digital age, emails have become the lifeblood of communication for businesses of all shapes and sizes. But let's face it, not everyone is a pro at crafting emails that get results.

That's where this book comes in !

I've packed this guide with all the insider tips and tricks you need to elevate your email game. From writing killer subject lines to nailing the perfect tone, I've got you covered. I'll also show you how to write emails for different scenarios, like networking, job applications, customer service, and internal communication. Plus, you'll learn how to use email marketing to grow your business.

But it's not all just about making your emails look pretty, we'll also delve into the importance of security and compliance when it comes to business emails. Don't worry, I'll make sure you're not breaking any rules.

So, whether you're a small business owner, a sales pro, or an executive, grab a cup of coffee, get comfortable, and let's start writing emails that will blow your recipients' socks off!

The BluePrint

The Basics

As you embark on this journey to master the art of effective business email writing, it's important to remember that just like building a house, crafting a business email requires a solid structure. In this book, we will take a closer look at the key elements of an effective email structure and provide you with tips and techniques to help you write emails that get results.

But before we dive into the details, let's take a moment to visualize the basic structure of a business email as if it were a house.

The subject line is the foundation of your email, it needs to be strong and clear to hold the weight of your message. The greeting sets the tone for the email and should be tailored to the recipient, it's like the frame of the house, giving the email its shape and style.

The body of the email should be clear, concise, and easy to read, like the walls of the house holding all the information and details.

The closing should summarize the main points, provide a call-to-action and include a polite closing, like the roof of the house, it protects the email and keeps it safe.

The signature and attachments should be professional and consistent with the tone of the email, like the finishing touches in a house, they add the final details and make the email complete.

Here's an example of a basic structure of a business email:

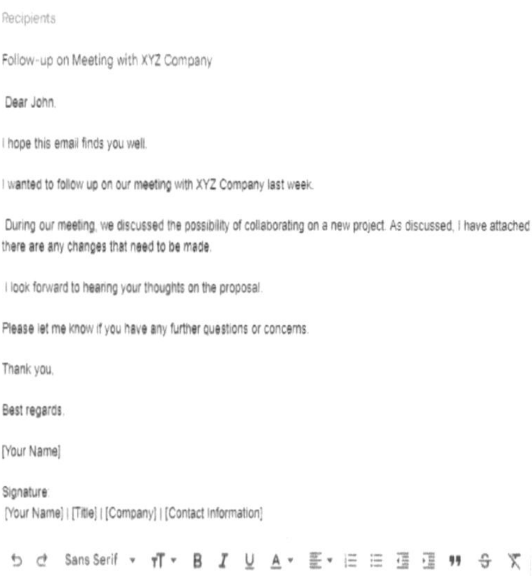

This example email has a clear and concise subject line, a professional and appropriate greeting, a clear and attention-grabbing opening, a well-organized and easy-to-read body, a polite and clear closing, professional signature, and an attachment that is mentioned in the body of the email.

By understanding and following this basic structure, you can ensure that your emails are clear, concise, and effective. And like a well-built house, your emails will stand the test of time and be sure to impress your recipients.

In the following chapters, we will take a closer look at each element of the email structure, and provide you with tips and techniques to help you write emails that get results.

So, put on your hard hat and let's get started on building the perfect email.

Chapter 1 The ABC of Email Writing

Welcome to the first chapter of our book on email writing for business !

I am excited for you to dive into the world of emailing like a pro. By the time you finish reading this chapter, you'll be a pro at crafting emails that get results. But before we dive into the nitty-gritty of email writing, let's start with the basics,the ABCs of email writing. A is for "Attention-grabbing subject line." B is for "Brevity is the soul of wit." C is for "Call to action."

A - Attention grabbing subject line.

As you sit down to compose your next email, you may be thinking, "What's the big deal about the subject line? My email content is what really matters."

But think again!

The subject line is the first thing your recipient sees, and it's often the deciding factor in whether or not they open your email.Just like a book cover or movie title, your subject line needs to be intriguing and attention-grabbing and when it comes to B2B and B2C businesses, the approach to crafting subject lines can be quite different.

But how do you do that?

Well, let's dive into the world of crafting killer subject lines.

B2B subject lines tend to be more professional and informative. They focus on providing value and addressing specific pain points or challenges that the recipient's business may be facing. They often use industry-specific language and terminology and may include statistics or data to back up claims.

For example:

- "Discussing Your Project's Progress and Next Steps"

- "Meeting to Review Your Business's Growth Strategies".
- "Upcoming Meeting to Discuss Your Business's Cybersecurity Measures"
- "Discussing Your Business's Growth Strategies and Next Steps"

On the other hand, B2C subject lines tend to be more casual and personal. They focus on creating an emotional connection with the recipient and often use more casual language, emojis, and persuasive words to grab their attention. They also tend to focus on the benefits the recipient will receive from the product or service rather than the features.

For example:

"Let's Talk About Your Dream Wedding"
Meeting to Discuss Your Home Renovation Needs"
"Let's Talk About Your Dream Vacation"
"Meeting to Discuss Your Health and Wellness Goals"

But before you move on, make sure to stick to these fundamentals:

1. Keep it short and sweet: Subject lines should be no more than 50 characters.

   A study by Radicati Group found that the average open rate for emails with a subject line of 28-39 characters was 58.4%, while emails with subject lines of 5-13 characters had an open rate of 66.8%.

2. Use action words: Use words like *"act now," "limited time," "final warning,"* etc. to create a sense of urgency.

3. Personalize the subject line: Use the recipient's name or company in the subject line to grab their attention.
4. Use numbers and statistics: Using numbers and statistics in the subject line can increase open rates.
5. Be specific: Be specific about what the email is about in the subject line, so recipients know what to expect.
6. Test different subject lines: A/B test different subject lines to see which one performs best.

So, whether you're a B2B or B2C business, have fun experimenting with different subject lines and see which ones work best for your audience.

B, brevity is the soul of wit.

In today's fast-paced business world, time is like a precious diamond and nobody wants to waste it reading long-winded emails. That's why brevity is the ultimate superpower in business communication. The saying "brevity is the soul of wit" applies to emails just as much as it does to speeches and writing.

When crafting an email, it's like building a puzzle, and you have to be concise and to the point throughout the entire message. A study by the University of Missouri found that emails with short and concise sentences are like the missing piece of the puzzle, making it more likely for recipients to understand the message and take action. Keep your email body like a snack, short and focused on one main topic, and break down complex ideas into smaller, easy-to-digest chunks. Avoid using unnecessary words or phrases, and get straight to the point like a sharp knife.

Personalization is another way to make your emails more engaging and increase engagement. A study by Experian found that personalized emails are like a warm hug, they had a 29% higher unique open rate than non-personalized emails. Use the recipient's name or company in the body of the email to make it more relevant to them, or just to make them feel special.

It's important to also be mindful of the tone and language used in the email. The use of action words such as "urgent" or "limited time" can create a sense of urgency, which can increase engagement. Using numbers and statistics in the body of the email can also be effective, as a study by MarketingSherpa found that emails that included numbers are like a winning lottery ticket, they had a higher open rate than those that did not.

By keeping emails short, sweet and to the point throughout the entire message, you increase the chances of your message being read, understood and acted upon. So, make sure you don't beat around the bush and always get to the point, unless of course you're telling a good joke!

C for Call to Action.

This is where you'll tell your recipient what you want them to do next. Whether it's to schedule a meeting, make a purchase, or just hit reply, make sure your call to action is clear and easy to follow.

Remember, Attention-grabbing subject lines, Brevity, and Call to Action. These are the building blocks of crafting an email.

When it comes to emails, a powerful call-to-action (CTA) is like a superhero's sidekick, it helps you save the day by getting your recipients to take the desired action. Whether you want your recipients to click a link, make a purchase, or register for an event, a clear and effective CTA is essential.

But, let's be real, crafting the perfect CTA can be a real brain teaser.

That's why it's important to make it stand out like a beacon in the night. Use action-oriented language and make it bold and prominent, like a bright red cape on a superhero. And don't be afraid to play with words, a clever pun or witty phrase can be a real attention-grabber, like a catchy tagline on a superhero's suit.

Another tip is to keep it simple, like a one-liner from a superhero. Avoid using complex language or technical jargon, and stick to clear and straightforward phrases like "Sign up now" or "Learn more." And don't forget to make it clear what the recipient will get out of taking the desired action, like a superhero's superpower.

It's also important to test different CTAs to see which one resonates best with your audience. A/B testing is like a superhero's sidekick, it helps you see which CTA is the real MVP. You can test different phrases, colors, and placement to see which one gets the most clicks.

A clear and effective call-to-action can be the difference between a successful email campaign and one that falls flat.

So, make sure to craft the perfect CTA and watch your recipients take action like a superhero saving the day!

There are several types of call-to-action (CTA) that businesses and marketers can use to encourage their audience to take a desired action. Some examples include:

1. **Button CTAs:** These are like the "big red button" on a control panel, just waiting to be pressed! Example: *"Shop Now"* or *"Learn More"* button on a homepage.

2. **Text CTAs:** These are like secret treasure maps, leading users to hidden pages full of goodies. Example: *"Read our blog"* or *"Sign up for our newsletter"* in a website's footer.

3. **Form CTAs:** These are like treasure chests, filled with valuable resources or special offers. Example: "Download our e-book" form on a landing page.

4. **Image CTAs:** These are like pictures on a treasure map, pointing the way to a specific landing page or product page. Example: A product image with a *"Buy Now"* button overlay on an e-commerce website.

5. **Video CTAs:** These are like the end of a treasure hunt, where you get to see the final prize and find out how to claim it. Examples: *"Subscribe to our channel"* or *"Visit our website"* at the end of a brand video.

It's important to note that the CTA should be specific and clear, and the action it promotes should be easy to complete. Also, it's good to test different types of CTAs and evaluate their performance to determine which one works best for your audience.

Can we have a CTA that just tells the customer about the next actions they are supposed to take ?

Yes, it is possible to have a call-to-action (CTA) that simply informs the customer about the next steps they should take, without necessarily prompting them to take a specific action. This type of CTA is often referred to as an "informational CTA."

An informational CTA can be used in situations where the customer has already taken a desired action and is now looking for guidance on what to do next.Informational CTAs can also be used in situations where the customer is in the research phase and wants more information before taking action.

For example: After a customer has made a purchase, an informational CTA might say:

"Congratulations on your purchase!

Your order has been received and is being processed. You will receive a confirmation email shortly with all the details. Track your order anytime by visiting the order tracking page on our website.

If you have any questions, please don't hesitate to contact us."

This CTA provides the customer with valuable information about the status of their order, and also guides them on how to track the order and get in touch with the company if they have any questions. This type of CTA is useful in situations where the customer has already taken a desired action, and is now looking for guidance on what to do next.

It's important to note that while informational CTAs provide valuable information to the customer, they should be used in conjunction with other types of CTAs that encourage the customer to take action, for example, providing a link to the order tracking page, and also a contact information or a button to contact the company.

It's important to note that while informational CTAs provide valuable information to the customer, they should be used in conjunction with other types of CTAs that encourage the customer to take action.

When creating your CTAs, make them clear and specific, and easy to complete, like a treasure hunt, easy to follow the instructions.

Also don't forget to test different types of CTAs, like trying different routes to reach the treasure, to determine which one works best for your audience.

Chapter 2   Tone Talk

The Importance of Sounding Right

Once upon a time, there were two young business people named Ria and Vijay. They both worked at the same company and were tasked with reaching out to potential clients. Ria had been working at the company for a few months and had already closed several deals. Vijay, on the other hand, was a new hire and was still trying to figure out how to be successful in his role.

Vijay noticed that his emails were not getting the responses he was expecting and decided to take matters into his own hands. He knew that he needed to find a way to write effective emails, so he decided to research best practices for business email communication. He read articles and books, and studied examples of well-written emails.

Through his research, Vijay discovered the importance of using simple and clear language, and how to match the tone of his emails to the context and purpose of his message. He also made sure to proofread his emails to ensure that there were no errors.

With his new approach, Vijay's emails started to get responses and he was able to close several deals. His supervisor was impressed with his progress and Vijay quickly became one of the top sales representatives in the company.

On the other hand, Ria, who had not been paying attention to the tone and language in her emails, started to see her performance decline. Her clients complained that her emails were too formal and robotic, and that they felt like they were talking to a machine rather than a human.
Ria soon realized the importance of tone and language in her emails and started implementing the same changes as Vijay.

The tone and language you use in your business emails can greatly impact the effectiveness of your communication with your clients. Think of it like this: you're trying to strike a balance between "I'm-a-serious-business-person" and "Hey-let's-grab-a-beer-after-work".

It's important to take the initiative and research the best practices for business email communication, like Vijay did, and to be aware of the tone and language you're using, and choosing them carefully to match the context

But, what exactly is tone?

Tone is the way in which you communicate your message. It's the attitude that comes through in your writing.

Here are some words and phrases that can be used to convey different tones in an email:

1. **Friendly tone:** "Great to hear from you", "Hope all is well", "Looking forward to working with you", "Thanks for your time", "Appreciate your help"

2. **Formal tone:** "Dear [Name]", "As per our discussion", "Regarding the matter", "I would like to inform you", "Please find attached"

3. **Persuasive tone:** "I strongly recommend", "It would be beneficial for you to", "You won't regret it", "Don't miss out on", "Exclusive offer for you"

4. **Confident tone:** "I am confident that", "I am sure that", "I can assure you that", "I am certain that", "I am positive that"

5. **Empathetic tone:** "I understand how you feel", "I'm sorry to hear that", "I appreciate your concerns", "I'll do my best to help", "Let me know if there's anything else I can do"

6. **Professional tone:** "Please let me know", "Thank you for your prompt reply", "I am looking forward to hearing from you", "As per our agreement"

7. **Casual tone:** "Hey", "What's up", "Catch you later", "Sounds good, man", "No worries"

In business emails, it's important to maintain a professional and respectful tone throughout the email, and avoid using overly casual language, slang, or emoticons.

One study found that emails with a conversational tone are like a scoop of cookies and cream - they're sweet, friendly, and build great relationships. Plus, they're more likely to be devoured (read) by the recipient!

On the other hand, emails written in a more formal tone are like a scoop of classic vanilla - they're dependable, trustworthy, and perfect for business-to-business communications.

In addition, A study showed that emails written in a positive tone are more likely to receive a response than those written in a neutral or negative tone, just like how a scoop of mint chocolate chip ice cream is more likely to be chosen over a scoop of plain vanilla.

Follow these hacks to get the tone of an email right :

- Start by understanding the purpose of your email and the audience you're communicating with. This will help you determine the appropriate tone to use.

- Use a friendly, conversational tone when writing emails to colleagues or clients you have a good relationship with.

- Use a more formal tone when writing emails to clients or colleagues you don't have a strong relationship with, or when discussing sensitive or important issues.

- Use a persuasive tone when trying to convince someone to take a certain action or make a decision.

- Use a confident tone when presenting information or making a request.

- Use an empathetic tone when addressing a problem or addressing concerns.

- Avoid using overly casual language, slang, or emoticons in business emails.

- Use the "sandwich method": Start with a friendly and positive opening, provide the main message in a clear and concise way, and end with a friendly and positive closing. This approach helps to maintain a positive tone throughout the email.

- Read your email out loud to yourself before sending it to ensure that the tone is appropriate and that there are no errors.

- Remember that your tone should match the context of the email, and always try to be respectful and professional.

- Use a Thesaurus: If you are struggling to find the right words to convey the tone you want, use a thesaurus to find synonyms that better fit the tone you want to convey.

Just like how you can mix and match different flavors of ice cream to create the perfect sundae, it's important to match the tone of your emails to the context and purpose of the message. And also don't forget to experiment with different tones, like trying different flavors of ice cream, to find the one that works best for your audience.

Bonus Tip 

Correcting the grammar and tone of an email is crucial for creating a professional and polished message. Whether you are communicating with colleagues, clients, or partners, a well-written email can leave a lasting impression and enhance your credibility.

Luckily, there are several tools available to help you ensure your emails are free of grammatical errors and written in an appropriate tone. One such tool is Grammarly, which is a popular grammar checking software that provides suggestions for correcting grammar, spelling, punctuation, and style. It also includes a tone detector that analyzes the words and phrases you use to determine the overall tone of your message and provides suggestions for improvement.

Chapter 3 The Art of Persuasion

Writing Emails that Win

Imagine you're in a negotiation, and you need to convince the other party to see things from your perspective. The same principles apply when writing persuasive business emails.

In this chapter, we will be diving deeper into the specific techniques of persuasion that can be used to make your emails more effective.

Whether you're trying to close a sale, schedule a meeting, or get buy-in for a new project, understanding and applying these techniques can make a big difference in the outcome of your communication.

We will be covering key persuasion techniques such as the Reciprocity principle, the Scarcity principle, Social Proof, the Authority principle, the Consistency principle, the Liking principle, and the Commitment and Consistency principle.

 Each technique will be explained and exemplified with examples of how it can be used in business email writing.

So, let's get started !

1.   **The Reciprocity principle:**

Let's put this principle into practice. Think of something you can offer your recipient before making your request. It could be a complimentary consultation, a free sample of your product, or even a valuable resource.

Write down your offer and keep it handy for your next email.

Example : *"I wanted to offer you a complimentary consultation before we discuss our services further. Would you be available for a call next Tuesday at 3 pm?"*

2. The Scarcity principle:

This principle is all about creating a sense of urgency. Try experimenting with different phrases and language to create a sense of scarcity like, *"limited time offer"*, *"only a few spots left"*, *"don't miss out"*. Take note of which phrases work best for your audience and use them in your emails

Example : *"Due to high demand, we only have a few spots left for our upcoming workshop. Don't miss out on this limited time opportunity!"*

3. Social Proof:

People trust what others say more than what you say. Gather testimonials, statistics and references to authority figures that you can use in your emails to add credibility to your message.

Try to include them in every email you send.

Example: *"97% of our customers have reported an increase in sales after implementing our strategies. See testimonials from satisfied clients on our website."*

4. The Authority principle:

Credibility is key. Research reputable sources in your field and use them to bolster your argument. Keep a list of credible sources on hand for reference in your emails.

Example : *"According to a recent study by the Harvard Business Review, companies that use our services see an average of 25% increase in revenue."*

5. The Consistency principle:

Consistency is key for building trust. Try to reference previous agreements or commitments in your emails to provide a sense of consistency.

Keep a record of previous conversations so you can refer to them in your emails.

Example : *"As we discussed in our previous conversation, I wanted to follow up on the next steps for implementing our plan."*

6. The Liking principle:

People like people who are similar to them. Try to find common ground with your recipient and use it to build rapport. Find something you have in common and mention it in your email.

Example : *"I hope this email finds you well. I noticed that we both share an interest in hiking. I recently went on a trip to Yosemite, have you ever been there?"*

7. The Commitment and Consistency principle:

Make it easy for your recipient to commit. Start with small commitments and build on them. For example, asking for a confirmation of interest before asking for a bigger commitment.

Example : *"We're excited to offer you a special deal on our service. Can you please confirm if you're still interested by replying to this email?"*

Activity: Tone, Language, and Persuasion in Action

Objective: To practice using tone, language, and persuasion techniques in real-world scenarios

Instructions:

1. Choose a scenario from the list below or come up with your own.
2. Write an email using techniques covered in the first three chapters of the book, including tone, language, and persuasion techniques.
3. Share your email with a friend, colleague, or mentor and ask for feedback on how effective it is in terms of tone, language, and persuasion.
4. Reflect on the feedback and make any necessary adjustments.

Scenarios:

1. You are a sales representative trying to schedule a meeting with a potential client.
2. You are a project manager trying to get buy-in from team members for a new initiative.
3. You are a marketing manager trying to increase attendance for an upcoming event.

Write down your final version below:

Chapter 4 Fine-Tuning Your Email

Sending an email may seem like a simple task, but have you ever sent an email and regretted it later because of a typo, a missed attachment or an unclear message?

In this chapter, we'll be taking a closer look at some simple but effective ways to fine-tune your emails before hitting send, so that you can be confident that your message is clear, concise and persuasive.

The Power of Proofreading:

When it comes to sending emails, we all want to make sure our message is clear, concise, and error-free. But, let's be real, proofreading can be quite a snooze-fest. But, don't worry, I've got your back with some fun and effective ways to proofread your emails!

One of my favorites is the backwards-reading technique. Start by reading the last sentence of your email and work your way to the first. This will help you focus on individual words and phrases, making it easier to spot errors like a pro.

Another tip is to use tools like Grammarly, Hemingway, and ProWritingAid which can help you identify errors quickly and easily. These tools can check for grammar mistakes, spellings, punctuation errors, and even suggest improvements to your sentence structure. Now, don't just rely on these tools, always get a second opinion, maybe even ask a friend to give it a read.

You can also proofread your emails on different devices, because let's face it, formatting and spacing can look different on different screens. And if possible, proofread your emails in a quiet and distraction-free environment, it'll help you focus and pay attention to details.

Lastly, proofread your emails at different times of the day, your brain processes information differently at different times, so you might spot errors you missed earlier.

What key aspects of an email require fine-tuning?

When crafting an email, it's vital to give extra consideration to several key components. These elements include the subject line, which sets the tone and expectations for the content within the email, the opening salutation, which establishes a friendly or professional tone and starts the conversation off on the right foot, the body content, which conveys the main message and supports the call-to-action, the call-to-action itself, which provides a clear next step for the recipient, and the closing, which leaves a lasting impression.

Furthermore, it's important to evaluate the overall tone, language, and format of the email to ensure that it is tailored to the recipient and the situation, thus increasing the chances of a successful outcome.

Test, test and test again:

When it comes to sending out emails, it's always a good idea to test them first before sending them to a large group. Imagine sending out an email with a typo in the subject line or a broken link, it could be a disaster!.

Try the "test group" technique. Send your email to a small group of people, it could be your friends, family or colleagues and ask them for feedback. This will help you identify any errors or issues before sending it to a larger group. Another tip is to test different subject lines, and you can even use tools such as SubjectLine, SubjectLine Tester or Omnisend to help you find the best subject line for your email.

Time is Essence:

The timing of when you send your email can have a big impact on its effectiveness. When it comes to sending out emails, timing is everything.

Have you ever sent an email at the wrong time and it got buried in the recipient's inbox? It's a bummer! But don't worry, we've got some fun and effective ways to make sure your emails land at the right time. You can use tools such as World Time Buddy to find the best time to send your email based on the recipient's location.

Another tip is to test the best days and times to send your emails. You can use tools such as MailChimp or Campaign Monitor to schedule your emails to be sent at the optimal time for maximum engagement. And don't forget, the day of the week matters too, research has shown that Tuesdays and Thursdays have the highest open rates for emails.

Follow-up like a pro:

In the game of business, following up is like the secret weapon in your arsenal, it might not seem like a game changer at first glance, but it can be the difference between sealing the deal and missing out. But let's be real, following up can feel like a chore. Don't let the burden of following up weigh you down, we have some secret weapons to make it easy and effective.

Let's start with the "reminder technique", set a reminder for yourself using tools like Boomerang or FollowUp.cc and you'll never miss a follow-up again.

Another tip is to add a sense of urgency by providing a deadline for the recipient to respond. And the key to success, include a clear and specific call-to-action in your follow-up email. With these tips, following up will be as easy as 1, 2, 3 and you'll be closing deals like a pro.

You've crafted the perfect email, but before hitting send, have you double-checked for spelling and grammar errors? Have you added a professional signature? Have you included some visual elements?

Fine-tuning your emails before sending them can mean the difference between a response and being ignored. Don't let your hard work go to waste, give your emails the royal treatment with some fine-tuning.

Think of it as a trip to the spa for your email, you give it a spell check massage, a professional signature manicure, and a formatting makeover. You even test it on different devices to ensure it looks and feels great on all platforms. And just like a spa day leaves you feeling refreshed and rejuvenated, fine-tuning your emails will give them that extra boost they need to stand out in a crowded inbox.

Is it necessary to fine-tune every email that I send?

While it's not necessary to fine-tune every single email you send, research suggests that taking the time to carefully review and adjust the content and formatting of your emails can significantly improve their impact and effectiveness. In fact, a study by the Radicati Group found that the average office worker sends and receives around 122 emails per day, making it increasingly important to make sure that your emails stand out and are well received.

Additionally, when it comes to emails that are particularly important or require a high level of response from the recipient, fine-tuning can be especially crucial.

By putting in the extra effort to make sure that these emails are well-crafted and effectively communicate your message, you can increase the chances that they will be read, understood, and acted upon.

Fine-tuning your may seem small, but it can make all the difference in how your message is received. Not only that, but you also establish yourself as a reliable and professional source of information, building a positive reputation in the process.

So, while it's not necessary to fine-tune every email you send, doing so can help you to get better results and make the most of your email communication efforts.Don't hit send without giving your emails the fine-tuning they deserve and watch your response rate soar!"

Chapter 5 Navigating Difficult Waters

How to handle tough emails ?

Difficult situations are an inevitable part of any business and when it comes to handling them through email, it can be even more challenging.

Whether it's dealing with a complaint, responding to a rejection, or handling a sensitive issue, the way you handle these situations can have a significant impact on your relationship with the customer and your business as a whole.

In this chapter, we'll explore some strategies and tips for handling difficult situations through email, with examples to help you navigate these tricky waters.

Handling Customer Complaints:

When a customer expresses a complaint, it's important to respond quickly and professionally.

The key is to address the issue, apologize for any inconvenience, and offer a solution. Before crafting your response, take a step back and try to see things from the customer's perspective. Understanding their point of view will help you craft a response that addresses their concerns and leaves them feeling heard and satisfied.

For example:

Dear [Customer],

We understand how frustrating it can be when [issue they are complaining about], and we apologize for any inconvenience this may have caused. We take your feedback seriously and have taken steps to resolve the issue. We have [what you have done to fix the problem].

As a gesture of goodwill, we would like to offer you [discount/coupon/gift card] as a token of our apology. Please let us know if there is anything else we can do to assist you.

Thank you for your patience and understanding.

Best regards,
[Your Name]

Responding to Rejection:

Rejection can be tough, but it's important to remain professional and gracious in your response. Instead of focusing on the rejection, use it as an opportunity to learn and grow. Businesses that ask for feedback and use it to improve their product or service tend to have better customer retention rate .

Ask for feedback and use it to improve your product or service.

For example:

Dear [Customer],

Thank you for considering our proposal. We understand that it may not be the right fit at this time, but we appreciate the opportunity to work with you. We value your feedback and would be happy to discuss any areas where we can improve in the future.

We would be grateful if you could take a few minutes to provide us with some feedback about our proposal. Your input will help us to improve our service and better meet your needs in the future.

Please keep us in mind for any future projects, and we wish you all the best in your endeavors.

Best regards,
[Your Name]

Handling Sensitive Issues:

When dealing with sensitive issues, it's important to use a professional and empathetic tone.

Show that you understand the customer's feelings and that you are willing to help. Use words that convey empathy and understanding.

For example:

Dear [Customer],

We understand that this is a difficult and sensitive situation. We are here to support you and do everything we can to assist you during this time. Please let us know how we can help and we will do our best to provide a solution.

We understand that [issue they are facing], and we want to assure you that we are here to help in any way we can.

Please don't hesitate to reach out to us if you need any further assistance.

Best regards,
Your Name

I know it can be tough to handle such emails ,but it's important to keep a clear head and remember the key strategies for success. By approaching the situation with a level-headed and organized mindset, you can effectively navigate even the most challenging emails.

First, take a moment to gather your thoughts and approach the situation with a calm and composed demeanor. This will help you respond in a measured and professional way.

Next, try to understand the sender's perspective. By putting yourself in their shoes and considering their point of view, you can respond in a way that is empathetic and understanding.

When crafting your response, be direct and clear in your communication. Avoid being vague or ambiguous, and ensure that the sender knows exactly what you expect of them.

In the event that the email pertains to an error made by you or your team, take responsibility and apologize for any inconvenience caused.Maintaining a professional tone and avoiding confrontational language or personal attacks is crucial. Remember, it's always better to address a difficult situation in a professional and respectful manner.

Lastly, keep detailed records of the email exchange, in case the situation escalates and becomes a dispute. This will provide you with evidence to back up your case and help you navigate the situation effectively."

By using a professional language and adding an interesting and engaging perspective, it can help the reader to remember the points better and it can make the information more appealing.

Chapter 6 Zero Inbox

Do you ever feel like your inbox is controlling you, rather than the other way around? Are you tired of being buried in a never-ending sea of emails, struggling to stay afloat and be productive?

In this chapter, you will embark on a journey to reclaim control of your inbox and transform it from a source of stress and distraction into a well-oiled machine that helps you be productive and focused.

The Science behind Overflowing Inboxes

Do you constantly feel like you're drowning in a sea of digital tasks and notifications? You're not alone. Studies have shown that the constant barrage of emails can have a negative impact on our stress levels, focus, and productivity.

Constantly checking our inbox and switching between tasks can result in "task switching overload", causing us to experience this.

In fact, it has been estimated that the average person spends 28% of their workweek managing emails and, and it's not uncommon to feel overwhelmed and stressed as a result.

The root of the problem lies in our brains' ancient "fight-or-flight" response. When we receive an email, our brains perceive it as a potential threat or task that needs to be handled. This triggers the release of stress hormones, like cortisol, and activates the fight-or-flight response.

Over time, the constant release of these hormones can lead to chronic stress, decreased focus, and decreased productivity.

How do I achieve Zero Inbox Nirvana ?

Zero Inbox is more than just an empty inbox - it's a state of mind. It's a philosophy that encourages regular processing, organization, and review of emails to free up your mental bandwidth, reduce stress, and increase focus. And with the right tools, it's easier than you might think.

Achieving Zero Inbox is both an art and a science. It requires a combination of practical strategies, tricks, and tools to streamline your email management process and keep your inbox organized and clutter-free.

1. Keyboard Shortcuts: Using keyboard shortcuts can save you time and increase your efficiency when processing emails. Some of the most useful shortcuts include "Archive" (to move an email out of your inbox and into your archive), "Mark as Read/Unread" (to quickly change the status of an email), and "Delete" (to quickly delete an email).

2. Automating Repetitive Tasks: Automating repetitive tasks, such as filtering and organizing emails, can free up your time and increase your productivity.

3. Leverage productivity tools: There are many tools available to help automate your inbox. For example, Boomerang can schedule emails to be sent later, or return to your inbox if you don't receive a reply.

4. Another tool, IFTTT (If This Then That), allows you to create custom automations based on triggers and actions.

5. The Two-Minute Rule: if an email can be completed in two minutes or less, do it immediately. By taking care of small tasks as soon as they arrive, you can keep your inbox organized and prevent them from piling up and becoming overwhelming.

6. Turn off Notifications: Turn off email notifications during designated "no-email" times to reduce the constant stimulation of the fight-or-flight response and increase your focus and productivity.

7. Email Management Apps: Use email management apps, such as SaneBox or Unroll.me, to simplify your inbox and keep your emails organized. These apps can help you sort your emails, categorize them, and automatically filter out spam, promotional emails, and other irrelevant messages.

8. Take advantage of email templates: Responding to common inquiries can be time-consuming. Create templates for your most frequently sent responses and save them for quick access. You can insert placeholders for specific details, such as the recipient's name or a date, to make each email personalized.

Unlocking the Power of Zero Inbox

Imagine a world where your inbox is empty, your to-do list is manageable, and your stress levels are low. This world is not a pipe dream, it's the world of Zero Inbox.

Here are the benefits of embracing this lifestyle :

1. The Productivity Boost: Say goodbye to the days of constantly switching between tasks and losing focus. With Zero Inbox, you'll eliminate distractions and increase your focus, allowing you to be more productive and get more done in less time. Picture yourself breezing through your to-do list with ease, and that extra free time you'll have to enjoy life!

2. Work-Life Harmony: Imagine a world where you can leave work at work. With Zero Inbox, you'll set clear boundaries between work and personal life, reducing stress and increasing your sense of balance. No more checking your emails at midnight, no more being "on" 24/7.

3. A Stress-Free Mind: Overflowing inboxes can trigger feelings of anxiety, stress, and overwhelm. By achieving Zero Inbox, you'll reduce the constant stimulation of the fight-or-flight response, increasing your sense of calm and reducing stress. Think of it as a mental spa day every day.

4. Uninterrupted Focus: Zero Inbox allows you to focus on the task at hand, reducing distractions and increasing your overall productivity. When you're able to focus, you're able to work more effectively and get more done in less time. Say hello to a new level of focus, clarity, and efficiency.

5. Creativity Unleashed: A cluttered inbox can be a major source of stress, reducing your ability to think creatively. By achieving Zero Inbox, you'll eliminate distractions and increase your focus, freeing up your mind and allowing you to be more creative. Think of it as unleashing the full potential of your imagination.

6. Embracing Zero Inbox is like unlocking a secret superpower. You'll experience increased productivity, better work-life balance, improved mental health, enhanced focus, and increased creativity.

So, are you ready to join the Zero Inbox revolution?

Chapter 7 Inbox Invasion

Building effective email campaigns

Email campaigns are like a superpower for businesses. They allow you to reach out to your target audience with laser precision, generate leads and boost sales with minimal effort. But, as you may already know, creating a successful email campaign requires a bit more than just sending out a few emails. It requires careful planning, effective design, and the use of automation and tracking tools.

With the right strategy, you'll be able to make a lasting impression on your target audience, and stand out from the competition. In this chapter, I'll reveal the secrets to creating email campaigns that will make your business thrive.

In this chapter, you will discover the secrets of planning, designing, and executing successful email campaigns. I will take you through the process of identifying the goals and objectives of your campaign, segmenting your audience for maximum impact, and creating a content calendar that will keep your emails on track.

I'll also share our best practices for designing effective email templates that will stand out in the inbox and grab the recipient's attention. And if you thought automation was just for big companies, think again !

You will see how small businesses can use automation and triggering to send targeted, timely emails. Finally, we'll explore different ways to track and measure the success of your campaigns, so you can use the insights you gain to improve future campaigns and take your business to the next level.

Planning your email Campaign

Here is a step-by-step process for planning a successful email campaign:

Step 1: Define your campaign's goal and objectives like a pro

- Start by determining the overall goal of your campaign. Are you looking to increase website traffic, boost sales, or build brand awareness? Having a clear goal in mind will help you create a campaign that is focused and effective.
- Next, set specific, measurable objectives that align with your overall goal. For example, if your goal is to increase website traffic, your objectives might include: increasing the number of click-throughs to your website, increasing the number of new visitors to your site, or increasing the average time spent on your site.
- Once you have your goals and objectives in place, you'll be able to measure the success of your campaign by tracking key metrics such as open rates, click-through rates, conversion rates, and revenue generated.

Step 2: Segment your audience like a boss

- Segmenting your audience is an essential step in creating an effective email campaign. By dividing your audience into smaller groups based on characteristics such as demographics, behavior, or interests, you can create more targeted and personalized messages.
- For example, you can segment your audience based on:
    1. Demographics: Age, Gender, Income, Education

2. Location: Country, Region, City
3. Purchase history: Products bought, Amount spent, Time of purchase
4. Behavioral data: Email open rate, click-through rate, website visits
5. Interests: Products they have shown interest in, events they have attended, etc.

- By segmenting your audience, you'll be able to create campaigns that are more relevant and engaging to each group, which will increase the chances of the email being opened and acted upon.

Step 3: Create a content calendar like a wizard

- Creating a content calendar is a great way to plan and organize your email campaigns. It allows you to map out when each email will be sent, what it will contain, and who it will be sent to.
- A content calendar helps you ensure that your campaigns are consistent, timely, and relevant. For example, you can plan your email campaigns to promote a sale at the right time, with the right message, and to the right audience. This will increase the chances of the recipient engaging with the campaign and ultimately making a purchase.
- Additionally, you can use the content calendar to plan email campaigns for upcoming events, festivals, and holidays. This will help you be timely and relevant with your campaigns.
- Use tools such as Trello, Google Calendar, and CoSchedule to create a content calendar that integrates with your email marketing platform and make it more efficient.

Step 4: Create the campaign like a genius

- Use the segmented audience and the content calendar to create highly-targeted, personalized campaigns that are relevant and engaging to each group.
- Make sure your emails are visually appealing and easy to read, with a clear call to action.
- Test your emails before sending them to a small group of recipients and make any necessary adjustments.
- Tools like Canva, Adobe Spark, and BEE Pro can help you design visually appealing emails.

Step 4: Create the campaign

- Use the segmented audience and the content calendar to create highly-targeted, personalized campaigns that are relevant and engaging to each group
- Make sure your emails are visually appealing and easy to read, with a clear call to action.
- Use tools like Canva, Adobe Spark, and BEE Pro to design visually appealing emails.
- Test your emails before sending them to a small group of recipients and make any necessary adjustments.

Step 5: Monitor the campaign

- Track key metrics such as open rates, click-through rates, conversion rates, and revenue generated
- Use the data to optimize future campaigns

- Don't be afraid to experiment with different elements of your campaigns, such as subject lines, email content, or calls-to-action to see what works best.
- Use tools like Mixpanel, Omniconvert and Google Analytics to monitor the campaign.
- Excel sheet tricks like creating charts and graphs can help you visualize the data and make informed decisions.

Designing your email campaigns

Are you tired of creating lackluster email campaigns that fail to engage your audience?

Look no further! With the right tools and tricks, you can design email campaign templates that are not only professional-looking but also highly engaging.

One of the best tools to use when designing email campaign templates is a template builder. Platforms like MailChimp and Constant Contact offer a wide range of templates that you can customize to suit your needs, including templates for newsletters, promotional emails, and more. Plus, with their easy-to-use drag-and-drop features, you don't have to be a coding expert to create stunning templates.

But let's not forget the importance of keeping it simple. Your audience's attention span is limited, so avoid using too many colors, fonts, or images. Stick to a clean, simple design that will make it easy for them to focus on your message. And with more and more people accessing emails on their smartphones and tablets, it's crucial to make sure your email is responsive. Many template builders offer responsive design templates that will ensure your emails look great on any device.

Before hitting the send button, make sure to test your template. Tools like AWeber's Inbox Preview and MailChimp's Inbox Preview allow you to see how your email will look on different devices and email clients, so you can make any necessary adjustments. And to really make your emails stand out, consider personalizing them.

Personalized emails have been shown to increase engagement and improve open rates. Platforms like MailChimp and Constant Contact make it easy for you to segment your list and send different emails to different groups of people based on their interests or behavior.

So, don't settle for mediocre email campaigns anymore! With the right tools and tricks, you can design emails that are both professional and engaging, guaranteeing that your message reaches the right people at the right time.

Email Campaigns for Manufacturing Businesses

Woo Hoo! Are you ready for some serious email campaign inspiration? Because I've got some inside scoop on how to make your manufacturing business stand out! As someone who has spent time in the manufacturing industry, I know the ins and outs of what works and what doesn't.

So, let's dive in and make your email campaigns fun, engaging, and effective!

1. **New Product Launch:** Get your customers excited about your latest innovation by announcing the launch of a new product through an email campaign. Include high-quality images and a detailed description of the product, as well as information about its features and

benefits. Offer a special deal, like a discount on the first purchase, to entice customers to buy.

Example: "Introducing our new innovation in personal care products - made with science backed ingredients to give you the best results. Order now in bulk and enjoy a 10% discount on your purchase!"

2. **Industry News and Insights:** Keep your customers informed about the latest industry trends and developments by sending emails that provide updates on industry news and insights into how your company is adapting to these changes.

Example: "Stay ahead of the game with our latest industry insights. Discover the latest advancements in automation technology and how our company is leveraging them to streamline our manufacturing process, like Tony Stark building a new Iron Man suit.

3. **Case Study:** Share your company's success stories by highlighting the positive impact that your products and services have had on your customers. Use case studies to showcase your company's expertise and reputation in the industry.

Example: "See how our company helped XYZ Manufacturing increase their production by 30% with our custom-designed machinery. It's like a manufacturing fairy tale, with a happy ending for everyone. Read our case study now."

Here is an example of how a business can use email marketing:

A small retail store that sells clothing wants to increase sales and promote its new collection. To do this, they decide to use email marketing. The first step is to build an email list. They do this by setting up a sign-up form on their website and in-store, and they also collect emails from customers during check-out.

Next, the store creates an email marketing campaign to promote the new collection. They use images and descriptions of the new clothing items, and include a special discount code for the email subscribers. They also include a clear call-to-action, such as "Shop now" to encourage recipients to make a purchase.

To make the campaign more effective, the store segments the email list based on customers' previous purchases. They create different versions of the campaign for customers who have previously bought casual clothing, formal clothing, and accessories. This way, the store can target the specific product to the customer's interest.

The store schedules the campaign to be sent out on a specific date and time, and then sends it to the email list.

After the campaign has been sent, the store tracks and analyzes the results. They use tools such as open rate, click-through rate, and conversion rate to measure the success of the campaign. Based on the results, they can make adjustments to future campaigns to improve their performance.

Make sure your campaigns should be visually appealing, informative, and provide a clear call-to-action, all while being entertaining. They should also be segmented based on the recipient's interests, so that the most relevant information is sent to the right audience.

Chapter 8 Power of Email Templates

Gone are the days of spending countless hours crafting the perfect email. With email templates, you can communicate effectively and efficiently, all while maintaining a professional and personal tone.

From layout to language, every aspect of your email has the power to impact your open rates and engagement. With the right strategy, you can go from blending in with a standard 20% open rate to shining with an impressive 80% open rate.

To help you elevate your email marketing campaigns and sales outreach, we'll analyze various templates, breaking down what makes each one tick. By examining the key elements of successful emails, from the subject line to the signature, we'll give you the tools you need to craft messages that cut through the noise and drive results.

Welcome Email

A welcome email is a chance to strengthen newly established connections with your first-time subscribers. It serves as a way to introduce your brand and give your readers an idea of what your company is all about. It also sets the tone for future communication by showcasing your tone of voice.

It's important to continually tweak this email to align with your evolving brand and target audience. Make sure it effectively conveys your message so that your business leaves a positive first impression.

Use the provided welcome email template as a starting point and customize it to suit your specific needs.

Here's a template that works for both B2B and B2C businesses:

Subject: Welcome to [Brand Name]!

Dear [Name],

We're thrilled to have you as a new member of the [Brand Name] family! We understand that you have a choice in who you do business with, and we're honored that you've chosen us.

At [Brand Name], our goal is to [insert brand value/mission]. Whether you're looking to [insert reason for subscribing for B2B businesses] or [insert reason for subscribing for B2C businesses], we're here to provide you with the best possible experience and support.

In the coming weeks and months, you can expect to receive [insert what they can expect to receive from your business, such as newsletters, promotions, new product updates, etc.].

Our goal is to keep you informed, inspired, and connected to all that [Brand Name] has to offer.

In the meantime, feel free to explore our website and learn more about what we do. And, as always, please don't hesitate to reach out if you have any questions or need assistance with anything.

Thank you for choosing [Brand Name]. We're looking forward to a long and successful partnership.

Best regards,
[Your Name]
[Brand Name] Team

Sales Email

The purpose of a sales email is to grab the attention of the recipient, establish a connection, schedule a sales meeting, arrange a phone call or move forward with the next step. It's crucial to thoroughly research and understand the challenges and needs of your prospects before sending sales emails.

By showcasing your ability to bring value to their daily routines or solve their problems, you increase the likelihood of receiving a response.

And if you're worried about your emails getting lost in the inbox, don't be! Including a follow-up email can increase your response rates by up to 192%! and that is why i've included a follow-up email template to enhance your chances of success.

Subject: [Unique value proposition/ Pain point addressed] at [Brand Name]

Dear [Name],

I hope this email finds you well.

I came across [prospect's company/website] and was impressed by the work you do in [relevant industry]. At [Brand Name], we specialize in [unique value proposition/ pain point addressed].

We understand that [insert specific pain point] can be a challenge for many [B2B or B2C target audience], but with our [product/service], we've been able to help numerous businesses/consumers [insert specific results].

I would love the opportunity to discuss how [Brand Name] can help [prospect's company/you] address this issue. Would you be available for a quick call next week?

Thank you for your time and consideration. I look forward to the opportunity to connect.

Best regards,

[Your Name]

Follow up Email

Don't be discouraged if your first sales email goes unnoticed or is forgotten. A follow-up email can be the key to starting a conversation and forming a relationship with a prospect or lead. It's a great opportunity to re-engage and make a lasting impression.

Here's an effective Follow up email

Subject: [Brand Name] Follow-Up: Let's Connect About [Unique Value Proposition/Pain Point Addressed]

Hi [Name],

I hope this email finds you in good spirits.

I wanted to touch base regarding the [value proposition/pain point addressed] we discussed earlier and see if there have been any updates or developments.

I understand that [prospect's company/you] may have a lot on your plate right now, but I'd like to offer my support and see if there's anything I can do to help. Our [product/service] has helped many [B2B/B2C] businesses like yours [achieve specific results/solve specific problems], and I'd be thrilled to have the opportunity to share how it could do the same for [prospect's company/you].

If you're interested, I'd be happy to schedule a convenient time for us to chat more about how [Brand Name] can be of assistance.

Thank you for your attention and consideration. I'm looking forward to hearing back from you soon.

Best regards,

[Your Name]

Confirmation Email

A confirmation email isn't just a boring old notification that your order has been received. It's a golden opportunity to make your customer feel heard and valued.

By sending a confirmation email, you can reassure your customer that their order is being handled with care and that you appreciate their business.

But why settle for just a confirmation email when you can go above and beyond and offer your customer a little something extra?

Adding an incentive, such as a discount or free shipping on their next order, can not only delight your customer but also increase the chances of repeat business.

So why not make the most of this opportunity and turn a simple confirmation email into a valuable customer engagement tool?

Here's an example of a confirmation email that both B2B and B2C businesses can use:

Subject: Your [Business Name] Order Confirmation

Dear [Customer Name],

We just wanted to take a moment to thank you for choosing [Business Name]! We're thrilled to be a part of your [product/service] journey.

We wanted to confirm that your order [Order #] has been received and is being processed.

Rest assured, we're working hard to get your [product/service] to you as soon as possible.

In the meantime, if you have any questions or concerns, please don't hesitate to reach out. Our customer support team is here to help!

As a token of our appreciation, we'd like to offer you [discount or offer] on your next purchase with us.

Simply use the code [discount code] at checkout.

Thank you again for choosing [Business Name]. We can't wait to see the positive impact [product/service] will have on your [business/life].

Best regards,

[Your Name]

[Business Name] Team

Review Email

Picture this: Your customers rave about their experiences with your business, sharing their positive thoughts with the world. The impact is massive. Not only does it boost your brand's reputation, but it also helps you attract even more customers.

So, what's the secret to getting more reviews?

Timing. Strike the right balance between sending the review email too soon and too late. Send it too early, and your customers may not have enough information or experience to form a solid opinion.

Wait too long, and their memories may have faded. Here's an example which will help you understand better.

Subject: We'd love to hear about your experience with [Company Name]

Dear [Customer Name],

We hope this email finds you well.

We wanted to take a moment to thank you for choosing [Company Name] for your recent purchase. We strive to provide the best products and services to our customers, and we hope that we have exceeded your expectations.

We would be truly grateful if you could take a few minutes to share your experience with us. Your feedback is invaluable and helps us continue to improve and provide a better experience for all of our customers.

If you're willing, please take a moment to leave a review on [Company's review platform].

If you've already left a review, we thank you for taking the time to do so.

Thank you again for your business and support. We look forward to serving you again in the future.

Best regards,

[Your Name]
[Company Name]

The ideal time to send a review email is when the experience is still fresh in the customer's mind and they have had enough time to fully understand the value of your products or services.

The sweet spot is typically within a week or two after the transaction.

Timing is key, so choose wisely!

Bonus Tip 

If you use Gmail for email communication, you can take advantage of its templates feature to quickly insert pre written content into your emails.

To create a new email with a specific format and content, simply click on the three dots in the top right corner of the compose window and select "Save draft as template." From there, you can access your saved templates anytime you need to send an email by clicking on the three dots and selecting "Insert template."

My Thoughts

Drafting emails can be intimidating, but having pre-made templates on hand can simplify the process. If you frequently send a specific type of email, such as an employee referral or webinar invitation, consider creating a template to improve the chances of your email being opened and receiving a response.

So, get those creative juices flowing and make your next email an interesting and impactful one!

Chapter 9   Are Emails Legally Binding ?

You send emails all day, every day, but did you know that each one of those messages could be a legal landmine waiting to explode?

That's right, emails can carry the same legal weight as written contracts, which means that every time you hit "send," you're potentially putting your rights and obligations on the line.

In this section, we'll dive deeper into the legalities of emails, from the binding power of emails to the importance of protecting sensitive information in your emails.

Additionally, I'll share some practical tips and tools to help you stay compliant and protect yourself from potential legal trouble.

Whether you're a business owner, a professional, or just someone who regularly sends and receives emails, you'll find valuable information in this chapter.

So, read on to learn everything you need to know about the legalities of emails!

In the eyes of the law, an email exchange between two parties that contains an offer and acceptance of that offer is considered a binding agreement. This means that if you make a commitment in an email, you could be held to it just as if you had signed a written contract.

This legal principle applies to a wide range of agreements, from simple promises to perform a service to complex business deals. As long as the email contains the essential elements of a contract, such as offer, acceptance, and consideration, it can be considered legally binding.

But how do you know when an email is legally binding?

The answer is not always straightforward, and it depends on the specific circumstances of each case. Essentially, an email can be considered legally binding if it satisfies certain requirements such as offer, acceptance, and consideration. This means that if you make an offer via email and the other party accepts the offer, you have entered into a legally binding agreement.

This applies to both personal and business emails, so it's crucial to be mindful of the language you use in your emails and to understand the potential consequences of your actions.

It's also important to remember that emails are considered written evidence, and they can be used as evidence in a court of law. This means that if you're involved in a legal dispute, your emails may be used as evidence against you.

To ensure that your emails are legally binding, you should follow some basic guidelines, such as:

- Be clear and concise in your communications

- Include all the essential terms of the agreement, such as the parties involved, the subject matter, the terms and conditions, and any relevant deadlines

- Use a professional and business-like tone

- Offer and acceptance: In order for an email to be legally binding, there must be a clear offer made by one party and an acceptance of that offer by the other party.

- This can be demonstrated in an email through the use of language such as "I offer to sell you X for Y dollars," followed by a response of "I accept your offer to sell X for Y dollars."

To protect yourself, it's a good idea to keep a record of all your emails and to be mindful of the information you include in your emails, especially sensitive information such as confidential business information or personal information.

Chapter 10 The Ultimate Email Sanity Check

Before you hit the send button, take a moment to review your email to make sure it's professional, clear, and error-free.

Here's a comprehensive checklist to help you send the best possible emails.

- **Verify the recipient:** Double-check that you have the correct email address for the intended recipient and that it is not a typo.

- **Re-read for clarity and tone**: Read your email over to make sure it is clear and that your tone is professional and appropriate.

- **Check for grammatical errors:** Grammatical errors can detract from the professional image you want to convey, so take a moment to review your email for typos and grammatical mistakes.

- **Attachments:** Ensure all attachments are properly added and labeled, and the recipient has the necessary software to open them.

- **Review the subject line:** Make sure the subject line accurately reflects the content of your email and will grab the recipient's attention.

- **Cc and Bcc:** Double-check the recipient list to make sure you have included all the necessary individuals in the "To," "Cc," and "Bcc" fields.

- **Consider a delay:** If the email contains sensitive information, consider using the delay send feature to allow for a second review.

- **Consider confidentiality:** Check if the email contains sensitive information and if necessary, use encryption to secure it.

- **Take a break:** If you're feeling overwhelmed, take a break and come back to your email with fresh eyes.

- **Confirm, then send:** Double-check all your items before hitting send. Make sure you're satisfied with the content, tone, and organization of the email, then send with confidence.

Activity : Spotting Errors

Instructions:

Read the following email and try to spot as many errors as you can:

Subject: Urgent Request

Dear Sir/Madam,

I hope this emal finds you well. I am writing to request you assistance with a urgent matter. Our compeny is having trouble with our shipment and we need it resolved as soon as possiple.

Could you please take a moment to call me back at (123) 456-7890 to discus this further?

Thank you for your time and I look forward to hear from you soon.

Best regards,

[Your Name]

Once you have identified the errors, rewrite the email below to make it professional and error-free:

*You can find my version of the answer on page 93

Chapter 11 The Great Debate

Email vs. Other Communication Channels

As the business world evolves, so do the ways in which we communicate. Email, once considered the king of business communication, is now facing tough competition from a host of new players.

But is email still the reigning champion, or has it been dethroned by the likes of instant messaging, social media, video conferencing, and more?

In this chapter, we'll delve into the heated debate and determine which communication channel reigns supreme in the business world. Get ready for a showdown as we pit email against its challengers and see which one comes out on top.

The Pros of Sticking with the Old Reliable

Email may be a classic, but it's still got some serious moves up its sleeve. Here are the advantages that make it a top pick for many companies:

1. Worldwide Access: With email, you can reach anyone, anywhere, at any time. This makes it a perfect fit for businesses with a global reach.

2. Easy Peasy: Email is simple and intuitive, requiring no special training to use effectively.

3. Time's on Your Side: With email, recipients can respond at their leisure, making it a great choice for non-urgent or complex discussions.

4. Document Dream Team: Emails can be saved, searched, and retrieved with ease, ensuring that important information isn't lost in the ether.

The Pros of Switching it Up with the Challengers

Here's why these new players are worth considering over the traditional email:

1. Instant messaging is lightning fast compared to email's snail-paced response time. With services like Slack, Microsoft Teams, or WhatsApp Business, you can communicate in real-time and get the answers you need without the wait.

2. Video conferencing offers a virtual face-to-face experience that beats the stuffy conference room any day. With services like Zoom, Skype for Business, or Google Meet, remote teams can connect in a way that feels just as real as an in-person meeting.

3. Instant messaging is all about brevity - with a focus on single thoughts or ideas, you can get your point across quickly and effectively. But the real magic lies in the conversational nature of instant messaging, allowing you to collaborate and connect with your colleagues in real-time.

My thoughts

When it comes down to it, the choice between email and other communication channels in business comes down to your specific needs and goals.

Email may be a tried and true option, but instant messaging, video conferencing, and social media each offer unique advantages that can make them a better fit for certain situations.

In some cases, the best solution may be to use a combination of communication channels, leveraging the strengths of each. For example, instant messaging may be ideal for quick, informal conversations, while email is better for longer, more complex discussions.

Video conferencing may be a great option for virtual meetings, while social media can be valuable for marketing and branding efforts.

Ultimately, the key is to stay informed about the available communication channels and their capabilities, and to choose the one that will best help you achieve your business objectives.

The communication landscape is constantly changing, and staying ahead of the curve can give your business a competitive edge. So, choose wisely and may the best channel win

Chapter 12 From Theory to Practice

Insights from real businesses

Email Marketing Success: The Amazon Way

Amazon's success is nothing short of remarkable.

But have you ever wondered what sets them apart from the competition?

The answer is simple: their culture of innovation. And it's not just in terms of their product offerings or delivery methods - Amazon's email marketing strategy is also a major contributor to their success.

By using clear and concise language in their transactional emails, such as order confirmations and shipping notifications, they keep their customers informed and engaged with their purchases.

But they don't stop there, they also use personalized recommendations in their promotional emails, utilizing customers' purchase history and browsing behavior to recommend similar products that customers might be interested in.

This approach not only increases the chances of a customer making a purchase, but it also helps to boost sales. By constantly innovating and improving their strategies, Amazon has managed to become one of the largest e-commerce companies in the world, with over 237 million active customers and a dominant market share in the world.

Who knew that a simple email could be so powerful?

When it comes to email marketing, Amazon doesn't play around. They know that your inbox is a sacred space and they don't want to waste your time with irrelevant messages. That's why they use personalized templates that are tailored to your behavior as a customer.

Whether you're new to Amazon or a loyal shopper, you'll get an email that's designed to make your shopping experience as smooth as possible.

And the best part?

The more you shop with them, the more they learn about you, so the emails keep getting better. They even include some extra information that's not essential but could entice you to explore more of their site. It's like a treasure hunt that leads to more sales!

Amazon has sent over 200 million welcome emails, and it's clear that they've nailed the perfect balance between useful information and marketing messages. From the very first email, they're able to connect with customers on a personal level and guide them towards a purchase. This is the power of email marketing, and Amazon is a master at it.

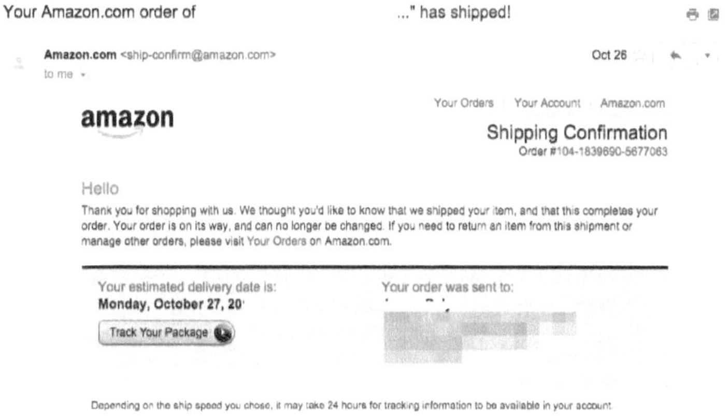

They use a combination of personalization, automation and data analysis to send highly targeted and effective messages to their customers. First, they segment their email list into different groups, such as new customers, repeat customers, or customers who have abandoned their shopping carts. This allows them to send tailored messages that are most relevant to each group.

Next, they use automation to trigger certain emails based on customer behavior. For example, if a customer abandons their shopping cart, they may receive an email reminding them of the items they left behind. They also use this strategy to cross-sell and upsell products to their customers that are likely to be interested in them based on their previous purchases.

But it's not just about sending emails, Amazon also tracks and analyzes the performance of their campaigns. They use metrics such as open rates, click-through rates, and conversion rates to measure the effectiveness of their strategy.

The E commerce giant isn't afraid to get personal with their customers through email. In fact, they embrace the opportunity to connect and drive results. Instead of relying on a one-fits-all approach, they constantly test and refine their email campaigns to find the sweet spot of frequency that maximizes returns.

One particular strategy that has proven successful for their customers is the use of a two-pronged email campaign for cart abandonment. By sending a follow-up email 24 hours after the initial message, they've witnessed conversions skyrocket by 50% or more. This just goes to show that a little extra effort can lead to big rewards.

In short, their email campaigns are a masterclass in targeted marketing. They use data, automation, and testing to deliver personalized and effective messages that drive engagement and sales.

How Netflix Dominates the Streaming Scene ?

As the king of the streaming world, Netflix reigns supreme while competitors like Disney+ and Prime Video are hot on its heels. With OTT services becoming a ubiquitous part of our daily lives, it's impressive that Netflix continues to lead the pack.

But it's not just their massive collection of original content that keeps them on top - they've also perfected the art of email marketing. From acquiring new subscribers to retaining loyal ones, Netflix has redefined the way streaming platforms approach email campaigns.

So what's their secret?

Netflix is a firm believer that email marketing is far from dead and still holds significant relevance.Say goodbye to bland emails that end up in the junk folder and hello to exciting, high-quality content.

The streaming behemoth is continuously testing innovative and unique strategies to get the best results from this marketing channel.

Want to learn from the experts? Here are five secrets to Netflix's email marketing success:

1. Netflix offers tailored movie recommendations based on each user's viewing history, location, and even pausing or fast-forwarding habits. With 33 million different versions of the platform, they track every user's viewing patterns to create personalized personas reflected in the emails received.

2. Subject lines play a crucial role in email marketing and Netflix knows how to create subject lines that truly engage their users and boost their opening rate. By sending "Top 10 in…" and "Trending" emails, they tap into the popularity of a series or film to generate new subscribers and reignite interest among existing users.

3. Netflix performs 250 A/B tests per year to determine which emails perform best, using machine learning to create better segmentation and more relevant emails for the user. They analyze large data sets to determine if changes to the email improve conversion rates and create a more personalized campaign for each customer.

4. Netflix knows how to make the most of holidays and special events by sending emails with horror-themed series for Halloween and Christmas film suggestions. They know how to take advantage of these events and create an enjoyable email experience for their customers.

it's no longer just about binging your favorite shows, it's about the data driving it all.

Answer - Page 82

Now, let's review the errors in this email:

1. In the first sentence, "emal" should be "email."
2. In the second sentence, "compeny" should be "company."
3. In the third sentence, "possiple" should be "possible."
4. In the fourth sentence, "discus" should be "discuss."
5. The salutation is not personalized, it should be "Dear [First Name]" or "Dear [Title and Last Name]."
6. The signature is missing the sender's title and full name.
7. Vague Subject line

After inculcating the above changes, here's how the email should look like:

Subject: Urgent Request :Shipment Tracking or *Assistance required for Shipment Tracking*

Dear [First Name],

I hope this email finds you well.

I am writing to request your assistance with an urgent matter. Our company is having trouble tracking our shipment and we need it resolved as soon as possible.

Could you please take a moment to call me back at (123) 456-7890 to discuss this further?

Thank you for your time and I look forward to hearing from you soon.

Best regards,
[Your Full Name]
[Your Title]

By practicing spotting errors in emails, you'll be able to write more professional and effective emails in the future.

Keep up the good work!

My Key Takeaways:

Congratulations on reaching the end of this journey towards a more productive inbox!

By following the tips and techniques outlined in this guide, you now have the tools and knowledge to take control of your email and achieve inbox zero. Whether you're a busy professional, a small business owner, or just someone looking to streamline their email process, this book has something for everyone.

Emails are no longer a source of frustration, but a tool for success.With a productive inbox, you can conquer the world one email at a time.

So, let's raise our virtual glasses to a brighter future and endless possibilities!

Thank you for reading!